**Crafts of the World**

# Japanese Origami: Paper Magic

Ann Stalcup

The Rosen Publishing Group's

**PowerKids Press** ™

New York

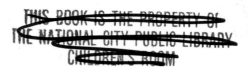

To my husband, Ed, who shares my love of folk art and travel

Special thanks to Joseph Wu for his origami expertise.

Published in 1999 by The Rosen Publishing Group, Inc.
29 East 21st Street, New York, NY 10010

First Edition

Book Design: Resa Listort

Photo Credits: pp. 4, 8, 11, 17, 18 by Joseph Wu; p. 7 © Keren Su/Corbis; p. 12 © Travelpix/FPG International; p. 15 © Roberto Arakaki/International Stock; p. 16 © Miwako Ikeda/International Stock; p. 19 © Gridley, Peter/FPG International; pp. 20-21 by Christine Innamoroto.

Stalcup, Ann, 1935-
      Japanese origami : paper magic / by Ann Stalcup.
          p.      cm. — (Crafts of the world)
      Includes index.
      Summary: Describes some specific origami figures and their significance in Japanese culture. Includes directions for creating an origami ornament.
      ISBN 0-8239-5333-5
      1. Origami—Juvenile literature. [1. Origami. 2. Japan—Social life and customs.] I. Title. II. Series: Crafts of the world (New York, N.Y.)
TT870.S675 1998
736'.982—dc21                                                                                          98-3876
                                                                                                           CIP
                                                                                                            AC

Manufactured in the United States of America

# What Is Origami?

Origami is a Japanese form of art in which squares of paper are folded to create shapes. You can make animals, flowers, or anything else you can imagine. Each origami shape or creature has a special meaning. Most origami figures are made from one square of paper. And you don't have to cut or glue in origami.

Origami is part of Japanese **culture** (KUL-cher). This special craft is passed down from **generation** (jeh-nuh-RAY-shun) to generation. Origami was first created for special **ceremonies** (SEHR-eh-moh-neez). Now it is done mostly for fun and decoration. Many Japanese people believe that origami teaches **patience** (PAY-shunts) and **concentration** (kon-sen-TRAY-shun).

Origami shapes, such as these cranes, can be made from paper of one color, or paper with patterns.

# Cranes: *Tsuru*

Cranes are tall, beautiful birds. In Japan, cranes are called *tsuru*. It is believed that giving 1,000 origami cranes to someone will allow him or her to make a wish. Cranes are also thought to have special healing powers.

In 1955 a twelve-year-old Japanese girl named Sadako Sasaki was very sick. She had gotten sick because of a bomb that was dropped on Japan in 1945, during World War II. Sadako believed that she would get well if she folded 1,000 origami cranes. So she folded and folded. Sadly, Sadako finished only 644 cranes. Her friends and family made the rest.

Sadako made the whole world see how cruel war can be. Today, a statue of Sadako stands in a park in Japan. This statue stands for peace. People from around the world leave origami cranes at the statue's feet.

Because of Sadako Sasaki, origami cranes have become a sign of peace. ▶

# Contents

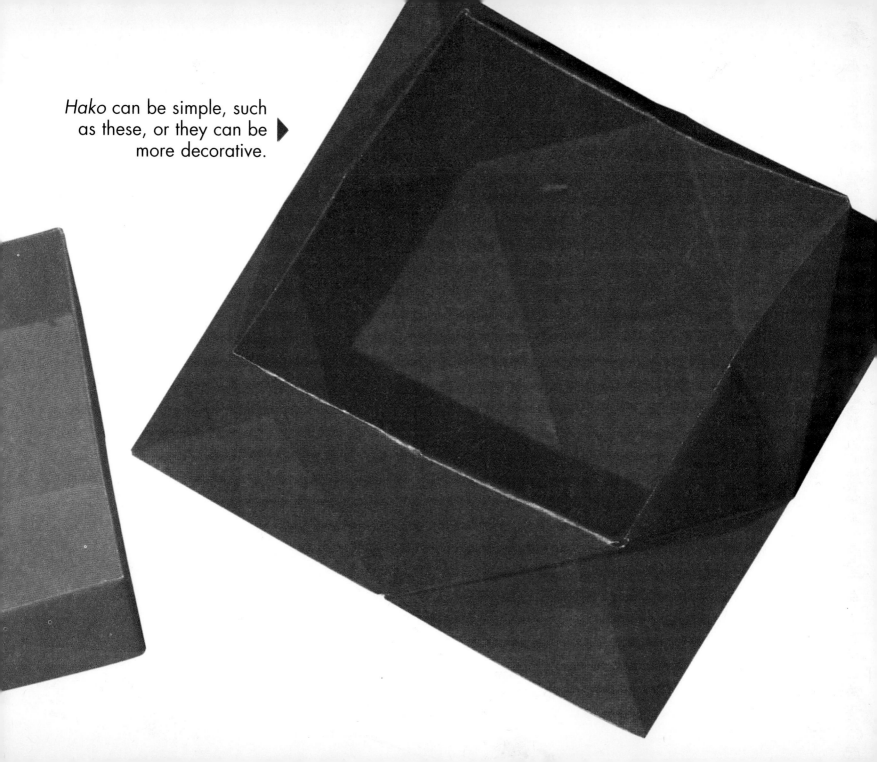

*Hako* can be simple, such as these, or they can be more decorative. ▶

# Frogs: *Kaeru*

In Japanese culture frogs are thought to bring luck. The Japanese word for frog, *kaeru*, also means "to return." One meaning of the word "return" is to get something back, such as money.

Some Japanese businesspeople carry an origami frog in their pocket when they go to meetings. They believe this will bring them luck and good **fortune** (FOR-chin). Frogs heard singing by a pond are also thought to be lucky. Some people believe that singing frogs bring needed rain.

◀ If you gently press on the back of an origami frog, you can make it hop.

# Boxes: *Hako*

Giving gifts is an important part of Japanese culture. And the gift wrap, called *tsutsumi*, is as important as the gift itself. A lot of care and thought go into choosing the *tsutsumi*.

Some gifts are wrapped in large cloths tied in a special way. This is called a *furoshiki*. Other gifts may be placed in handmade origami boxes, called *hako*.

Origami boxes are always **appreciated** (uh-PREE-shee-ay-ted). When you give a gift in an origami box, it shows that you took time to design and make the gift wrapping yourself. Making a gift beautiful shows **respect** (re-SPEKT) to the person whom you are giving it to.

# Doll's Festival: Hina Matsuri

March 3 is a special holiday in Japan. It is called Hina Matsuri, or the Doll's Festival. This is a special day when mothers and daughters show handmade dolls to their friends and family. Many young girls also show special dolls that belonged to their mothers or grandmothers. These dolls are placed on special shelves, made just for them. A prince doll and princess doll sit on the top shelf, and musicians and other dolls sit below them.

Origami princes, princesses, and musicians are also made to celebrate Hina Matsuri.

This is a very special day for Japanese girls. They wear their most beautiful robes, called kimonos. Their friends and family visit to see the dolls and to share sweet rice cakes.

◀ Hina Matsuri is a day that honors Japanese girls.

# Carp: Koi

May 5 is Boys' Day, a festival for boys. A special **symbol** (SIM-bul) of Boys' Day is the koi, or carp. A carp is a kind of fish. In school, boys often make origami carp. They talk about why carp are an important symbol. Carp are fish that swim up streams and waterfalls against strong **currents** (KUR-ents). To the Japanese, carp symbolize strength, **courage** (KUR-ij), and success.

On Boys' Day, families fly kites shaped like carp, hoping that their sons will grow up to be strong and brave. Kites are flown from bamboo poles. The largest, highest kite stands for the oldest son in a family.

These long strands of koi help the Japanese celebrate Boys' Day. ▶

# Helmet: *Kabuto*

On Boys' Day, boys dress like **samurai warriors** (SA-muh-ry WOR-ee-yerz). And like girls during Hina Matsuri, the boys have special dolls on this day.

Often, on Boys' Day, origami helmets called *kabuto* are made. Some helmets fit small origami warriors. Other helmets are made large enough for the boys to wear. Pretending to be warriors, the boys show how brave they are during make-believe sword fights.

Boys' Day is now known as Children's Day. Although boys are honored most, all Japanese children are taught how important courage and bravery are.

◀ Families celebrate together on Children's Day.

# Iris: *Shobu*

The word *shobu* means iris in Japanese. Irises are tall flowers that are usually white, yellow, or purple. But *shobu* also means **competition** (kom-peh-TIH-shun). Because *shobu* means these two things, irises have become a symbol of Boys' Day—the day when boys need to show their bravery. On Boys' Day, boys take baths with irises in the water. Origami irises are also made for the boys.

The origami irises are difficult to make and are almost as beautiful as the real flower.

Not only do the Japanese use irises to stand for battle, but they have also **adopted** (uh-DOP-ted) the Chinese belief that irises keep bad things away.

People like to learn how to make origami irises ▶ because they symbolize many different things.

# Tanabata Matsuri

## You will need:

2 or 3 squares of origami paper (or thin colored paper)
  6 inches by 6 inches, or 7 inches by 7 inches.

**note:** construction paper is too heavy for this project.

A piece of yarn or heavy string, about 3 yards long.

**1.** Fold the square in half and then half again. Unfold it.

Fold the square diagonally, then unfold it.

Fold the square diagonally the other way, then unfold it.

**2.** Fold the square along the first crease you put in it and push the top side corners into it, forming a triangle.

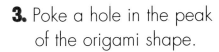
**3.** Poke a hole in the peak of the origami shape.

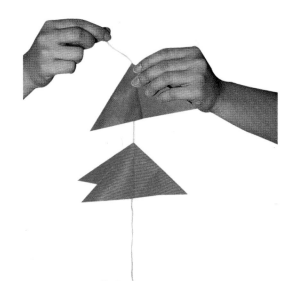

**4.** Push the yarn through the top of the triangle and string the triangles on the yarn.

# The Star Festival: Tanabata Matsuri

The Star Festival, Tanabata Matsuri, happens on July 7. It celebrates the make-believe story of love between two stars. Vega, the Weaver Princess, and Altair, the Herdsman, were in love. They thought only of each other and forgot about their jobs. Altair let his herds wander, and Vega didn't weave. The king got angry at Vega for not weaving, so he separated Vega and Altair. The king said that they could meet only once a year, on July 7.

Every July 7, Japanese people make origami stars and hang them from rooftops and ceilings. These stars stand for the night sky. They remind people of the story of Vega and Altair.

The special meanings connected to origami creations have lasted for thousands of years. People all around the world have learned how to make origami. By creating origami pieces, the world keeps a beautiful Japanese **tradition** (truh-DIH-shun) alive.

# Glossary

**adopt** (uh-DOPT)  To take something that is not your own and make it your own.

**appreciate** (uh-PREE-shee-ayt)  To be thankful for something or someone.

**ceremony** (SEHR-eh-moh-nee)  A special act or series of acts that are done on a certain occasion.

**competition** (kom-peh-TIH-shun)  A contest to see who is the best at something.

**concentration** (kon-sen-TRAY-shun)  Paying very close attention to something.

**courage** (KUR-ij)  Bravery.

**culture** (KUL-cher)  The beliefs, customs, art, and religion of a group of people.

**current** (KUR-ent)  The force of water traveling down a river or stream.

**fortune** (FOR-chin)  Wealth, riches, health, and good luck.

**generation** (jeh-nuh-RAY-shun)  The time (usually about 30 years) between parents and the birth of their children.

**patience** (PAY-shunts)  The ability to wait calmly for something.

**respect** (re-SPEKT)  To think highly of someone.

**samurai warrior** (SA-muh-ry WOR-ee-yer)  A soldier in ancient Japan.

**symbol** (SIM-bul)  Something that stands for something else.

**tradition** (truh-DIH-shun)  A way of doing something that is passed down through the years.

# Index